LOVE FLOWS

PETE FRIERSON

Order this book online at www.trafford.com
or email orders@trafford.com

Most Trafford titles are also available at major online book retailers.

Print information available on the last page.

ISBN: 978-1-4907-7035-2 (sc)
ISBN: 978-1-4907-7036-9 (e)

Library of Congress Control Number: 2016902758

Our mission is to efficiently provide the world's finest, most comprehensive book publishing service, enabling every author to experience
success. To find out how to publish your book, your way, and have it available worldwide, visit us online at www.trafford.com

Trafford rev. 02/19/2016

 www.trafford.com

North America & international
toll-free: 1 888 232 4444 (USA & Canada)
fax: 812 355 4082

CONTENTS

Acknowledgements

Love Flows is an extension of my two previous books, *Sweetness of the Heart, Mind and Soul* and the *Centerpiece of Love*. My writings are not meant to be a reflection of me, but of my thoughts.

Love Flows demonstrates clearly how the word Love can flow from the heart, mind, body and soul. Without love in our Life and without Love in the world, we are often left empty.

Love Flows can change things within the heart, mind and soul. Not to mention the effects real love has on our everyday living.

Sometimes there are things that we would love to say, talk about or just have an open discussion, but we are restrained because we do not know where to begin.

Love flows will guide, encourage and inspire you to the next level of enjoyment as human beings.

SPECIAL THANKS

Special thanks to Chantias Ford, Diane McFall, Laura Truelove, Diane James and Lorna McCandless-Moss for their dedication and input into making Love Flows a reality.

DEDICATION

This book is dedicated to all my siblings—John, William, Joe, Douglas, Alma, Billy, Randy and the late Clarence Frierson, Jr.

Special love to my grandchildren, Sydney, Siraj and Sanna'.

Thanks to all of my supporters who continue to support my endeavors.

Thanks to all my physicians, Dr. James Gore, Dr. Hrishi Kanth, Dr. Amit Choksi, Dr. J. Matthew Hassan, Dr. Aliya Frederick and the physicians at the Tennessee Valley Healthcare System.

This book is especially dedicated to the late Momma Betty Turner who transcended from this world to enjoy eternity forever. Also to her children, Jeffrey Turner and Regina Jamerson and her grandchildren, Justin and Alexis.

In Memory of Momma Betty

Mom is not gone. She has gone home to God's kingdom.

Betty, your gentle giant Dewey went home first to prepare for his queen and now you are on your way. What a reunion!

She was soft spoken, kind, considerate and well-respected and now her wings are on cruise control headed to meet her gentle giant.

Mom, you are not gone. You are in God's kingdom, the kingdom in the sky, where you shall never fear, never cry, never have another pain,

in that place that's the kingdom in the sky.

We will miss you dearly! Think of you often and sometimes we will even see you, but mom you are not gone.

Mom is not gone. She has gone home to that wonderful, peaceful and joyous place God calls home. She is not gone.

Mom lives on. Her words, her kindness, her tenderness and her strength shall live on. Mom is not gone. Her memories will carry you through.

Mom you are not gone. There will always be something that keeps you with us, a picture, a gift, a suit, a blouse, a dress or two, but mom you are not gone.

God took you to his kingdom, where there are no more tears, no more pain, no more sorrow, just joy so mom is not gone.

We will miss your Love, but we have all of your memories to carry us through. Mom you are not gone.

As the weeks turn into months, and months into years, your love mom, will always be with us no matter what.

Mom you are not gone... your life lives on in the hearts, minds and souls of all those you touched. Your love lives on.

LOVE FLOWS

Time comes, time goes
The message flows
down the veins, up the chambers and down to the heart.
Love flows. Words are expressed, feelings are on board,
Emotions flying around like snow.
It all comes together to show that love flows.
One night turned into a day, which then turned into days,
then weeks and now months – love flows.

MY INSPIRATION

You are my inspiration, north, south, east and west.

Without you in my life, I am lost. Wandering in a world of uncertainty,

you are my inspiration because you inspire a new life within me.

You give me the sparkle to smile. To walk a mile.

You are my inspiration.

You are my inspiration because God giveth and God taketh away,

but going forward, God gave me you.

You are such a warm delightful inspiration.

You are my inspiration because of your touch, your smile, the look in

your eyes and the way you take time out of your life to show me my weakness,

but at the same time, you inspire me to new heights.

My life changed the day we decided to be on the same page realizing

what we could or could not do.

You inspire me to want to live again, to live a full life and enjoy each day

with the inspiration of you in my heart, body and soul.

A gift from God...you may not realize even today why He sent you my way.

I cannot question what has happened, but I can follow your inspiration no matter

where it may lead me.

You are my inspiration for life and on this day,

I want you to know there will always be love for you from me.

Inspiration of life and inspiration of love, that's what you are to me.

WOMEN

Women are unique human beings and a woman would say that men are unique human beings as well. But a woman has her own uniqueness about her.
She has a way to make a person smile, make them happy and to share all the good things that God gave her.

Women can be the most lovable human beings that God ever created and when they are cultivated, nurtured, stroked, complimented and listened to.
A man's world becomes filled by the flagrancy of a woman's world or a woman's world becomes filled by the flagrancy of the man's world.

I don't care how you look at it... we cannot live without them.
Realizing that the world is changing and attitudes are changing too.
But, when you are from the "old school", you talk about a woman's world because this is the world in which the author of this book was raised.
I will say that women are unique human beings.

Women are sometimes more complicated than a computer and especially when you don't know anything about computers and I guess women would say the same thing about men. But sometimes, we are fortunate to find that unique woman and when that special woman appears from nowhere, all we can say is that she was God sent and when that happens, I want my readers to understand one thing, never, never let her go.

Without women in the world, men would be lost because women are the most unique human beings that God ever put on this earth and if you find one that you love, all I can say is love her to the very end.

I don't know everything about women, never have and never will, but I know I understand how women feel when they are loved, cared for, complimented, supported and given beautiful things in life. Women are unique human beings.

It's Something About You

It's something about you that I don't understand.
Maybe the answer is in your eyes or
maybe in your soul.
Either way,
it's something about you.
Maybe it's the way you look at me or the
way you touch me. Either way,
it's something about you.
I could dream for days and the answer would still evade me and I would sit and wonder...
it's something about you.
It's something about you that drives me wild inside.
Maybe it's your sweetness or your smile
that warms the heart, mind, body and soul.
Either way...
It's something about you that I don't understand, but in time... time will
reveal to me the true meaning of who you are and then I will understand
that special something about you that drives me wild inside.
It's something about you that I don't understand.
Maybe it's just you.

Your Eyes

Your eyes tell a story. A story of what your soul has endured.
Endured in so many ways. Endured in ways of much happiness.
Your smile and your laughter shine straight through my soul.

Your endurance of love is the inspiration to my soul and it inspires my heart to love you more.

Your endurance should be told in words yet to be spoken.
Your eyes are my soul—the gateway to my heart and the catalyst that keeps me whole.

Your eyes shine like gold and they will always be the gateway to my soul.
Your eyes… your eyes.

Your Touch

Your touch opened my heart to love. Your touch opened my emotions to desire. Your touch gave me new meaning to live. Your touch showed me what no one else has. Your touch is like sunshine on a cold day, it warms the heart.

Your touch, like a million dollars without the cash. Your touch reminds me of my first love. Your touch, without it, my heart would be lost. Your touch gave me the push that I needed to carry on. Even, in my darkest or weakest moments, your touch was felt within my soul.

Your touch, what does it really mean? Am I to really believe this is real or is it fantasy? Is it love or just an imaginary illusion of my thought process or my mind... for now, I am going to believe, that your touch is real.

She Stole The Show

The crowd was loud, full of anticipation about this and that, but she stole the
show. Her smile, her friendliness and her presence; she stole the show.
Dressed head to toe for the occasion, she stole the show.
The night is over, the awards are over and the laughter gone;
In the end though, she stole the show.
Her momma taught her well.
This here is how you steal the show.
"Dress, my dear, for the occasion" and that she did, that's how she stole the show.

TODAY

Today, as I begin my journey not sure where I am going or what I am going to do,
I do know today I shall smile and I shall warm a heart or two.
I shall have conversations because today is another day.
Today, I look at life different because it has so much to offer.
I turn tears into drops of gold.
I turn blood into a red steady flow of love.
Today will always be a day to be remembered.
A day to laugh, to smile, to think and to remember.
"What's so good about it?"
It is a day that God Almighty has made for us.
So on this day, just like every day I wake up, thankful that He has allowed me to rise.
I go to bed at night and I am thankful that He allowed me to go through the day.
Today, I am glad that you crossed my path and that you helped make today
what it is.

Roses are Red

Roses are red and your lips are too.
I can say in a million ways that I love you.
Roses are red and your lips are soft too.
Some days your lips remind me of the roses I sent you.
It does not matter because roses are red and each day that I think of you,
I am reminded of how deeply, I am in love with you.
Not afraid to say it too. I am sweet and reserved just like you.
But again, roses are red and we love each other too.

You Are Special

You are special to me because you are a special kind of person.
You are considerate and understanding.
You made me into what I thought I could never be.
You are special to me because of all of the things that you do. You listen when no
one else seems to care. You offer your opinion in the warmest way possible.
You show me compassion that has never been shown before.
You are special to me because I get up in the morning and I think about you.
I think about you and all of the things that I know that we could do,
plan to do and the things that we can dream about doing.
You are special to me because without you, there would never be a real me.
You are special to me.
You are special to me because you open the door to my heart that has been closed for
so long. You are patient with me as you try to show me that I am special to you too.
You are special to me because of your love, your thoughtfulness, your ability to
bring out the best in me and all of the other things that I did not see about me.
You are special to me.
You are special because God made you special.
I hope that as life would have it, you will see too that I am special
all because of you. Yes, you are special.

You Came into My Life

You came into my life and gave me life. You saw what others could not see.
You felt what others could not feel. You saw the need that others could not sense. You came into my life and you saw the outer appearance of happiness and on the inner side you saw unhappiness. You saw laughter, but the inner side,
you saw sadness. You saw boldness, but inside you saw confusion.

You came into my life and you gave me life. God sent you my way for whatever reason. Maybe it was to show me how to live, maybe it was to show you how to live. Either way, you came into my life. You gave me life.

You came into my life and you saw the pain of yesteryears tucked deep within my heart and you knew you had to find a way to change that hidden pain into happiness; that lost soul into life again. That confusion into boldness; that desire to be free into freedom and that desire to love again for however long... that's why you came into my life.

You came into my life and in the process, I gave you life. Life to see yourself like never seen before. Life to understand life's woes and to reflect on the past and say never again. You came into my life. You gave me life. We gave each other life.
Life to be joined together. Whatever the reason may be.

WE HAVE DREAMS

We have dreams and sometimes dreams are the only thing that keep us afloat. We dream about things that we never thought of and sometimes we dream about people we never heard of, but they are dreams. Dreams, we interpret in many ways and for some of us, it is an afterthought about something that may have happened in our life or it could have been something that happened today, yesterday or sometimes before. No matter how we look at it, it is a dream.

Dreams have many different points of view. We dream about winning something big. We dream about getting married and having children. We dream about going off to college and landing the most lustrous job in America. We dream about finding the right man or woman. We dream about success and how we make that happen. No matter how we look at life, without the ability to dream, we would be lost.

Dreams, sometimes we dream some of the most beautiful dreams in the world. Some have said that they have dreamed about what the afterlife is going to be like and have described that beautiful, beautiful place in the sky. Without the ability to dream, we would be lost.

Dreams sometimes are all that we have. Sometimes we wonder why we dreamed… what we did and sometimes we remember our dreams and other times we cannot remember anything about our dreams, but either way, we dream.

We dream daring to remember that everlasting activity of our memory.
Dream that is exactly what we do…daring to allow our minds to remember.
Dream, remembering what we did, what we saw and what we hope for.
Dreams… sometimes have an everlasting effect upon our minds.

Dreams—illusions of what can and cannot be. Dreaming is the sensation of the human thought process and the mind that's in deep thought or rest. Without dreams, we would be lost. Dream on my friend…dream on… because someday your dreams will come true.

THE PREACHER'S WIFE

The preacher's wife is a very interesting woman. Full of fun and not to mention all that energy that she has stored up inside, but what she might use it for is anyone's guess and I dare not ask. It's been said that she wore out one man and I dare not ask what that means, but that's the preacher's wife.

Quiet to most folks, but kind of wild when she is away from the limelight and I dare not ask because that's the preacher's wife. However, when she comes alive, she reminds you of a cougar, except she is all talk. Faithful and committed she is…that's her nature, but she is just the preacher's wife.

Known to make a person smile, laugh and can make a person come out of their comfort zone and I wonder how she does it. Maybe it is written in her DNA. Something that she is not sharing because after all she is the preacher's wife.

I think she has a way of getting whatever she wants, when she wants it and for however long she wants it, but that's the preacher's wife… what I just said. She is thrilling, exciting, adventurous and a lot of other things too. Now, I guess we will have to wait to read the next chapter of the preacher's wife life. After all, she is quiet until… I dare not ask, but again, she is the preacher's wife!!!

THE PASTOR SAID

The pastor said, at a recent home going celebration that "life is not over
when we transcend from this life to another life when we
are Holy in the Lord Jesus Christ's name."

The Pastor said, "When we die in the Lord Jesus Christ's name we shall rise again
and there are only two places in which we will spend eternal life." One of those is
with God in his kingdom in the sky and the other will leave us burning in hell.
The choice is yours.

The Pastor said, "The life that we are living while we are here is about
legacy. It is about memories. When you combine all of these, the true legacy
of your life is written. It is written before God or the devil."

The Pastor said, "When you are a Holy person you have no worries
because you know that the Lord will not forsake us."
The Pastor said, "When we are filled with despair, we know that the Lord will not forsake us".
The Pastor said, "He has preached at many funerals and that you can tell the
difference of whether someone was a person of God". Another preacher said,
"While I am a man of God, I am human too. I have feelings and I have emotions. I
build relationships just like you. When I lose someone I love, it hurts too."

The Pastor said, "When the phone calls quit coming, when the mail man stops delivering, when friends, coworkers and relatives quit coming by, when you are filled with despair, you call on the Lord."
The Pastor said, "When the tears begin to flow and you cannot control where they may fall, you call on the Lord."

The Pastor can be a man or a woman of God.

The Pastor said, "Just remember to look to the hills from where your strength comes from, when your heart is heavy and the tears are flowing from a loved one's passing, just remember to think of the Lord. If you do this, you will have an endless amount of joy."

THE FALL BREEZE

Sitting outside looking at the beautiful lake.
Just enjoying the fall breeze.

The birds are diving for food, wetting their wings and gliding across the lake.
I'm just enjoying the fall breeze.

The sound of the water beating against the shore reminds me of the mighty Atlantic
Ocean, it relaxes the mind.
I'm really enjoying the fall breeze.
The sun is beginning to set, there is a nice cool breeze cruising through the trees and
folks are walking, enjoying nature at her best.
I'm really, really ...enjoying this fall breeze.

Can't do much more, but relax and enjoy the fall breeze with Mother Nature at her best!
Wow... what a breeze.

MY RIDE

Today is different. She was warm, gentle, polite and interesting. Sitting in her chair, making eye contact with me as I begin my ride to recovery.

There is a conversation between the mind, the body and the soul. Slowly, we begin our ride; trying to figure out how to bring out old emotions and heal old wounds; replacing them with new ones or a compromise of the two.

Trying to stay out of the HOV lanes for now because if we go any faster it may cause a bumpy ride. My ride is like humpty-dumpty who sat on the wall, this time though; she is going to catch me... and I will be put back together with new desires, new emotions!

Sometimes this ride can be like a shattered piece of glass. Trying to put it all back together again hoping we don't miss a piece along the way.

Why She Loved Me

She fell in love with me because of my wisdom, my knowledge of life experiences, my caring and sharing attitude. She fell in love with me because I was there when she needed me. I was there in times of need, times of happiness and times of true understanding.

She fell in love with me because of my kindness, my desire to share knowledge, information, love, passion and her strong desire to build me up where I was weak.
She fell in love with me because of my strong need to show how to replace the negative ways of life with the positive ways of life.

She fell in love with me not for my money, rather for my warm and kind heart. She fell in love with me seeking, hoping and wishing for a future together for a better life. But in the end, all the love between us could not sustain our hopes and our dreams.

What Am I to Believe

What am I to believe when I know right from wrong? When I see you with two personalities. One that can make a person love another person, care for that person and be there for that person regardless. Your other personality questioning a person's motive and action. You say things and they never come true, so what am I to believe?

You are given the benefit of the doubt, given more chances than a cat with nine lives, given chances to explain your silence, yet your actions cause a person to ask, "What am I to believe?"

You tell me you love me and there has never been anyone like me. You tell me that you enjoy my company. You make me laugh and you make me smile. You give me the distinct impression that you are serious. But somehow in the end, I am feeling a betrayal of sorts, so I ask, "What am I to believe?"

The Love I Lost, But Couldn't Let Go

The love I lost, but couldn't let go was one that showed a commitment to love, to honor, to share a revelation of concern and a vision of I can't let go.

The love I lost, but couldn't let go had memories of years gone by. A love that was warm and compassionate from night to dawn. Excitement like never before. A heart beat that beats more than two. The love that I lost, but couldn't let go.

The love that I lost, but couldn't let go...there was a point and time in my life, I refused to let you go...years later,

I finally let go.

SUNSHINE

Sunshine, my dear, is the warmth of the sun's rays from God almighty!
It warms the blood, the heart, the mind and the soul. You are my sunshine my dear. In the morning, you are my sunshine; in the noon hour, you are my sunshine and in the night time you are my sunshine.

When I think of you... you are my sunshine. You make me feel brand new. You are the love of my life. Without your loving and tender touch, my life would feel so cold, but just knowing that you are my sunshine, brings a smile to my face and laughter to my soul.

You are my sunshine when I am down, when I am up and when I am going around and around, not sure of what's next except thinking of you. Hot, cold, rain or snow can never take the place of my sunshine.

I love you sunshine and you will always be the ray that shines in my heart, body, mind and soul!!!

Sometimes

Sometimes we love so much that we get nothing in return.

Sometimes we care so much... there is no more caring.

Sometimes we trust so much that the trust fades.

Sometimes we cry so much... there are no more tears.

Sometimes our emotions are filled with love and attachments; and other times they are empty.

Sometimes, we think there is hope and not wanting to give up, but we discover hope was an illusion of the mind.

Sometimes we wish for things or wanting something to happen and it does and other times it's like a beautiful Dove, gone in an instance.

Sometimes, we pray for this and that...sometimes our prayers are answered and other times it appears they were not.

Sometimes we want to see things for what we think they really are and later discover that it was nothing, but emptiness.

Sometimes our lives have to go on regardless of the circumstances or situations... sometimes with anguish and other times with no regrets.

Sometimes we are faced with so much at once that we don't know what to do, but to forge ahead one way or the other.

Sometimes we feel we are on this earth by ourselves, but we are not. The maker made us and He gave us the tools to survive. Some survive better than others, but either way sometimes we have to embrace life for what it is worth and sometimes we have to take a chance on hope and pray that we made the right decision.

Sometimes, we just have to live and put our trust and faith in God...knowing He will carry us through. Just sometimes...just sometimes.

If I Could Change Time

If I could change time, I would…not only for me, but for you. I would love you dearly and teach you what God taught me.

I would see the beauty in you, in your smile and in your touch.

If I could change time, you would always be first and foremost regardless of others.

If I could change time, you would be the Queen of my heart, the diamonds of my thoughts and the joy of my tears.

If I could change time, it would remain still as I touch you, love you and hold you like there was not going to be a tomorrow.

If I could change time…you would be there for me and I would be there for you. You are forever that sun that shines in my heart and the joy of my life. If only I could change time, I would…

Make Me Smile

Make me smile if you will. I have frowned for so long that I have forgotten how to smile. Make me smile if you will.

Make me smile when I look at you. Make me smile when I think of you. Make me smile when I see you laughing and joking around. Make me smile when I see the kindness beaming from your heart and your twinkling eyes. Make me smile.

Make me smile when you touch me. Make me smile when you say those three little words. Make me smile when you whisper in my ear. I know that my smile is a reflection of your beauty. Make me smile.

Make me smile. I have frowned for so long that I have forgotten how to smile. I haven't loved for so long that I have forgotten how to love. I have been afraid to let go and I have shielded my emotions from everyone. Make me smile.

Make me smile and I will make you smile in return. Love me and I will love you in return. Take care of me and I will take care of you all of the days of your life. I will make you smile. I will love you. I will take care of you. Every time I look at you, I will smile, smile and smile.

EYES

Eyes are like diamonds;

they sparkle like no other.

Eyes are the gateway to heaven.

Eyes are our ears.

Eyes are our sound.

Eyes see the beauty of life.

Without our eyes, we are lost in the dark.

Eyes, big, round, small, no matter what size, they can see into a person's heart.

Eyes are precious like gold.

Eyes can instantly show love.

They can spot things far away and can bring things close.

These eyes, must be cared for like Diamonds and Gold.

Without them, we are Lost!

These Eyes

Precious as Gold... these eyes.

My Life Changed Today

My life changed today when my heart was set free. Never dreamed I would fall so fast so quickly; but my life changed today.

My life changed today because someone came along and gave their heart and torched my soul.

My life changed today just knowing I found love where I never dreamed of before.

My life changed today and I will cherish each moment that I am given; never forgetting what I have and what can be.

My life changed today and I am very grateful to have my soul set free.
My life changed today.

THE EFFECTS OF

The effects of many aspects of life can go in many directions depending on the situation.

The effects of love can be exciting, fun, loving and just plain crazy, but the effect of love can also leave you devastated, angry, upset and much more.

The effects of trust can build a foundation so strong that a hurricane couldn't topple it, but when the trust is gone, it's like a roller coaster turning over and over again. The effects of mistrust can destroy the best laid foundation.

The effect of a good relationship is worth a million dollars without the money. It can bring such comfort to the heart, mind and soul, but when the effect of a good relationship goes sour, a person's world seems not worth living... that's how some folks feel about the effects of love, trust and a good relationship!

THINGS HAPPEN

For years, I heard the expression things happen. I often wondered what that really meant, but now I understand things happen.

Life can be great. Your smiles, your thoughts, your intentions and much more. All I can say is things happen.

Things happen sometimes without reasons or understanding. It can make the mind wonder- left to right or up and down. Either way things happen.

Things sometimes happen so fast that it's like a lightning rod... not sure where it will strike next. Things happen.

For the good or for the bad, things happen!

The Night Was Right

The night was right and the evening sensuous. Pretty as can be. We laughed and we shared a few tears of joy just knowing the night was right.

She realizes the love that I have for her and now the evening is set... she will love me and give me her best. The night was set. She showed her love for thee.

The night was right with all the trimmings and now you can only imagine what was left. The night was right.

Decisions

Decisions are something that we make in our everyday living. Sometimes, we make good decisions and other times not so good decisions. Sometimes, we make decisions based upon other people's opinions and other times not with enough information to say yes or no.

Sometimes, decisions are based on one person's perception. A decision based upon perception can be dangerous. Decisions based upon a person's gut feeling have a little more grit to it than most. Sometimes, we say that our decisions are made to protect us... is that a true statement or is it your way of taking control? You decide. Either way, it is still your decision.

Sometimes, we are influenced in our way of thinking because of something that may have happened to us in our lives prior to and when a new opportunity comes along, we can't see the trees for the forest and sometimes, we make judgmental decisions that are so wrong but that's how life goes sometimes. Decisions, once made, hardly ever can they be reversed!

We face decisions each day that we breathe God's fresh air. Sometimes, it could be a split decision or a decision that could devastate one to no end. It's easy to get into and a lifetime to get out of or even to correct that wrong. Sometimes, we hurt those that are our closest friends or love ones to the point... that a broken heart never mends.

Decisions are something that we cannot get away from or live without. However, when we come to a decision or decisions... we must always remember, it could have an everlasting impact upon those you love or those that you say you love.

Either way, they are your decisions. Good or bad, happy or sad... they all have consequences, so be ready to accept life's woes and live with your decision.

After all, they belong to you and not me. Decisions... a mega second can change your life forever. Been there and done that...

A Gift from God

A gift from God can come from many sources, many vessels and many avenues, so you see.

A gift from God can bring love happiness, quiet and tranquility to the heart, mind and the soul.

A gift from God is like no other. It can come from out of no-where. His vision you may not understand, but in time God's vision shall be revealed. A gift from God is what we all live for.

A gift from God, accept it, cherish it and be blessed within your heart.
He brings joy in the morning, midday, in the evening, all day and all night long.
Enjoy your gift!

I Am Always Right

I am always right no matter what I say, what I do, what I think or how I act.
In my mind, I am always right. I am always right in my thinking because I cannot be wrong. For I will ask a question to make sure that I have the answer, so that I can always be right.

I am always right is one lady's way of thinking. Sometimes we have to show a good lady that she may be often right, but not always right. But in her mind she is right.

Life is what it is. Most of the time, we are right. Other times we are not so right.
But I dare say that she was wrong.

There are some people in the world that are always going to be right even when they know they are wrong or even when they think they are wrong. To them, they are right. For us, who are sitting on the outside trying to get into that head of theirs, we too are convinced that they are right.

One might say...

I am always right. No matter where I go, no matter what I do, no matter the place, the time or the situation, I am always right. I am always right. When I am thinking, when I am sleeping and when I am dreaming, I am always right.

It would appear to me that you believe you are always right and there is no room for improvement. I dare not say that there is room for error because then I may be right. Do we meet halfway or do we want a war of who is right and who is wrong? Who may or who may not be RIGHT? In the end, no matter how we shake it, roll it or even think about it, you are always right. So I say to you, who believes that you are always right, we shall give you that honor. You are right.

You are my Friend

In the daytime or in the night... you are my friend.

When I am home with nothing else on my mind... you are my friend.

In the midnight hour and the bridge over troubled waters... you are my friend.

When I look at you and smile, flirt with you and call you something sweet...
you are my friend.

When times are hard, money is tight, jobs are scarce... you are my friend.

When I make mistakes or say the wrong thing or act the wrong way...
you are my friend.

No matter what I do or where I go... you are my friend.

Right or wrong, good or bad times... you are my friend.

Even when I want my friendship to turn into courtship and you say no...
you are my friend.

In the end, we are both unsure of what's right and what's wrong...
you are still my friend.

Silence is Gold

Sometimes, when we choose not to say anything,
the results are more powerful than speaking.
Silence is gold.

Sometimes, we are drawn into unpleasant situations, where we find
Silence is gold.

There will come a time in your life that you will have to make a decision to speak
or not to speak. You will have to decide to make noise or to be quiet.
To write or not to write, but either way...
Silence is gold.

There will come a time in your life that you will find peace within yourself,
but just knowing that you remained quiet is revolting to some... the world
is watching and waiting for you to make some noise and to express
whatever might be on your mind however to their disappointment.
Silence is gold.

Silence is gold when you try to read that person's mind.

That is, if you can and if you can't, you begin to look for their expressions to try
and get a read or a feel as to what they might be thinking. Sometimes, you might
get lucky and get a reading and sometimes you might get a false reading,
but you need to always remember,
Silence is gold.

Sometimes, we learn more by taking it all in and never speaking a word.
Sometimes, our enemies are thrown for a loop when they do not get a reaction of
sorts. It has often been said, "that every action does not call for a reaction."
I now, say to you, pick your place, your time and your situation so that
you too can say as I have often said in my life, "Silence is gold."

The Lady from LA

The softness of her voice, the gentleness of her tone, the laughter of her heart... it can only be the Lady from LA.

Seeking advice, she will express herself indeed sternly, yet so quietly. It can only be the Lady from LA.

Sparkle of her eyes, yet unseen, a twinkle here and twinkle there; a sparkle here or a sparkle there, it can only be the Lady from LA.

Given a few digits, punching a few numbers, asking what needs to be asked; position known on love, life, liberty and what the Lady from LA will or will not do... this is just another example of the Lady from LA.

Today, tomorrow, forever. Life is gentle. Life is rough. Life has its ups and downs; traveler she may be. But, sharing experiences can only be Lady from LA because she is the mystery lady that I have yet to see. The lovely Lady from LA.

Just listening to your laughter and sharing with me that you are fun, can only be the Lady from LA. A southern gal, you can learn to be; with your charm, along with the charm of a man who could light your fire. You will never again be the Lady from LA.

Soon, the Lady from LA will forget the ocean roar and settle for the misty sounds of the bird and the raindrops upon the rooftop. As the Lady from LA prepares to use that unforeseen mystery and that unforeseen talent that only the silkiness of that Lady from LA could unleash. The Lady from LA has traded her West Coast style for the charm of the southern mist. This is the Lady from LA.

My Daughter

My daughter is my heart. Born on the day MLK left this world. I knew I had a fighter. It's known that I love my daughter with all my heart. I will stand by her and I am her rock no matter what. In her lifetime, I can say we have only disagreed on things twice that caused a conflict. As life would have it, we worked our differences out and now we agree to disagree.

A daddy's love is different for a girl than the love for a boy. Either way, there is love. Her middle name, Tene', stands for love. The love of the human race, the love of family, the love of mom and dad, the love of big brother and the love that remains unspoken. Quiet in nature... that she is, but I can tell you, she has the fight of Martin and Malcolm too. She took that part from her daddy who taught her to believe in something and stand for what you believe in.

A daddy's love for his daughter cannot be matched by anything in this world. We live to see our children grow up to become whatever their heart desires and we support them the best that we can. We never forsake a day, a week, a month or even years because we can never turn back the hands of time.

I am proud to have a daughter like I do and I will tell the world that I will stand with and by you. I know what my role is in life toward you and I will never forget that I had a hand in bringing you into this old world too. You are my angel and you are my star. You have never caused me to take the walk of shame and I know deep down inside that you never will.

So, when the time comes and I am gone, remember all the things that we have done and never forget Tene', I love you with all my heart... from the man who taught you right from wrong! Love your father... your daddy.

Listen to Your Heart and Not Your Friends

Listen to your heart and not your friends because in the end, you will not win. Your heart will tell you if you are in love. It will tell you things that friends could never tell you. Listen to your heart and not your friends. Because, you will lose in the end.

Friends can try and tell you what they think, but are they really your friends or are they jealous of what you have or who you may be with?
Follow your heart.

It pumps, it beats, carrying love, happiness and peace. Listen to your heart.
It will tell you when it's time to stay, time to go or time to stand tall.

Listen to your heart and not your friends because in the end, you are not going to win.

Life is What It Is

We are born in this world in the image of God Almighty. As small as we may be, we grow, we learn and we communicate. We express ourselves. We share many things like love, affection and caring for one another...and that great sense of belonging with love and happiness.
As we travel the ways of life, we experience many things—some good and some not so good. We learn from self-preservation to protect ourselves as much as possible from the evils of the world. One of our greatest assets is our warm smile and warm heart. However, we still learn to cultivate those important lessons of needs, wants, desires, love and affection to the point where we discuss and realize what's right and what's not right. We learn to judge from someone actions. With these aspects, we pray along the way that God will give us strength to know and realize what *is* real and what *is not* real.
May we always strive for the joyous aspects of life, love, peace and happiness forevermore.

Life Is Too Short

Life is too short and when you love someone or someone loves you back, it's okay to say these words, "I love you, I miss you, I need you, I care for you and you mean the world to me" because life is too short. Life is too short especially when something serious happens. We then wish we could have said something special or meaningful to that person we loved so much.

Life is too short, so when you know you have something that really, really shows you all of those things written in this paragraph; return those words some way and somehow. Life is too short.

Life is too short and when the person you love or the person who loves you asks for a little reassurance of your commitment, thoughts or feelings, it has nothing to do with doubt. It's because one of those words-loving, caring, missing, needing, wanting, etc. has gotten out of line with the heart, mind and soul. It's up to you to put them back in line. After all, the heart, mind and soul all work together like one, two and three.

Life is too short. Never allow an opportunity to pass you by. If you can't say those words, then find a nice card that expresses your feelings. It is not about doubt; it is about keeping those words in line. Sometimes they want to move left, right, up or down, and it's our place to keep them in line. Life is too short.

So on this day, say something or do something to show the person you love, how a little reassurance of yourself means so much. Life is too short.
God giveth and God can take it away and that includes love, happiness, togetherness, trust and much more.
I am proud to tell you just how much I love you, need you and miss you because life is just too short. "I love you."

LIFE

Life is a place of being.

Hoping we can share moments of happiness on the highway or by-ways.

Life is so precious, yet taken so lightly. Today I love and tomorrow I'm gone.

Life is a place of being.

Life is like no other; once gone, it's gone. Somehow, we embrace the world around us, to laugh, to cry and sometimes jump for joy.

Life is a learning experience with the smell of roses or the sound of hard knocks.

Life is internal. For we find ourselves searching for our inner thoughts to see and remind us that we are human with love and with feelings, yet life remains internal.

Life is like folklore. It's what one chooses to make of it. Sometimes questioning our existence; yet we learn to roll with the punches and dance when there is music.

Life is everlasting. We live to create the memories of the yesterdays and the yesteryears to come. Life is filled with memories, stories, love, sadness, happiness, hope and the everlasting sense of "the untold stories." Life is today, tomorrow and the future.

Life is learning, life is internal, life is folklore, life is everlasting; life shall always remain.

Just Sitting

Just sitting and thinking about life. Sometimes, it brings a smile or two and other times it brings a frown to my face.

Just sitting and thinking about how different life can be and the changes that we have often experienced. Just sitting and thinking.

Just sitting and thinking about the yesteryears and the fun we had.

Just sitting and thinking, sometimes that is all that we have to do!

Old age brings about a change and memories is all that we have, so just sitting and thinking about life brings a smile to my face.

Just sitting and thinking.

I Thought About You

I thought about you last night with nothing else to do. As I was sitting in the
quietness reflecting back on life, you appeared on my radar screen and all
of a sudden I didn't know what to do. I thought about you last night.

I thought about you last night and it carried on through into the daylight. Today, I am
thinking about you. I don't know what it is about you, but last night I thought about you.

Could it be something we said? Or something we did? Or maybe the stars aligned themselves
in heaven above, so that you and I could think about each other as I did last night.
As life would have it, there are some things that cannot be erased. We focus on
the good things and we let the bad things go by. No matter how we look at it, I
can still say, "I thought about you" and, last night I thought about you too.
As the day starts and the day ends, the darkness begins to set as it once did; I want
you to know that last night, I thought and thought and I thought about you.

I Dream

I dream of the day that I can look into your eyes and see some joy.

I dream of the day that we can say, "we tried it without any regrets."

I dream of the day that I can see the smiles and the laughter of a wonderful person I know.

I dream of the day that I can hold you, feeling the warmth of your body and the smell that I love to smell.

I dream of the day that whatever we created will be with us forever.

I dream of the day that we can have some free moments together without any drama of any kind from anywhere.

I dream, I dream, I dream that our lives can be joined for whatever reason for however long and in the end, we know the true meaning of love.

I dream of the day that when I am gone and the wind is blowing, you will be the wind in my heart, the wind that's in my mind and the wind that's in my soul. You are the wind that keeps me going.

I dream that we can build something special that only you and I understand because it is not for others to understand.

I dream that I can understand someday why my love for you has been and still is so strong. In a world where you have, "We can't".

I dream finally that one day you will be the center of my life, my hopes and my dreams. No matter which road traveled, no matter where life takes you—know that there is one man who loves you, cherishes you and cares for who you are!

I SEE YOU

I see you like no other. I see you when you are happy. I see you when you are sad. I see the passion in you about what life is supposed to be about. I see the love that is within your heart and I understand the feeling and the hurt of a broken heart.
I see you.

I see you when you don't think that I am looking. I see you out of the corner of my eye. I see you in my heart with all of the laughter that you deserve. I see you in my soul because I know there could never be anyone else but you. I see you in a different light. I see you.

I see you in a way that no other man has ever seen you. I see you as someone who is warm, loving, considerate, trusting and very worthy of everything that God would want to take place between a man and a woman. I see you over and over again.

I see the beauty in your face. I see the beauty in your heart. I sense the beauty in your soul. I see the beauty that all others overlook.

I see you every day that I am breathing God's fresh air. I realize that the opportunity to love you, to care for you and to be with you is a once in a lifetime opportunity.
I see the beauty in you.

I see through the clouds and I bring sunshine. I see through the thunderstorms and I bring rain. I see through the cold weather and I bring warmth. I see through the tears and I bring joy. I see through the sadness and despair and I bring happiness. I see you like no other. You are the love of my life and the inspiration in my heart. Without you, I could not see. So, on this day, I want you to know that I can see the beauty in you.

I Love You

I love you each day that I smell God's fresh air. I love you because you care. I love you for the way you treat me and the way you show me love. I love you because of the way you touch me, the way you kiss me and the way you hold me.

I love you every day because it is the only way. I love you because you are my happiness, you are my joy and the inspiration that gives me hope. I love you because I see me when I see you and I see you when I see me. I love you for who you are. I love you because you bring the best out in me.

I love you because you are my world, my joy and my happiness. I love you because I just love you, you and you.

I Lost

I lost not because I did not love you. I lost because I loved you too much.
I lost not because I did not care. I lost you because I cared too much.
I lost not because I did not want you. I lost because I wanted you too much.
I lost not because I did not try. I lost because I tried too hard.
I lost not because I did not need you. I lost because I needed you too much.
I still need you in my life today.

Enjoy the Sun

Enjoy the sun, it's a lot of fun.
Fun to soak up, fun to feel.
Enjoy the sun, it warms the heart
and soothes the soul.
Enjoy the sun, cause tomorrow it might be cloudy.
Enjoy today's sun, tomorrow's sun and forever.
Just learn to enjoy the sun.

April Showers

As the saying goes... April showers bring May flowers. Such a sweet
appeal. It can cause the heart to flutter and the mind to go weak.
Just think, the raindrops of April showers bring lovely May flowers and
that's where you fit in. The thought of April showers can only bring
the smell of May flowers. Wow! What a wonderful smell!
April showers can be like you—beautiful from the beginning to the end.
April showers can bring a smile to your face and warmth to your heart.
Remember, April showers always bring May flowers. Remain as beautiful
as the May flowers and you'll never go wrong. Smile my dear.
April showers remind me of who? Just you!

I Am Ready

Today, I am ready to accept a new challenge. I know it will be different, but it is one that I chose. I must make the best out of it. I must leave all my bad habits behind. I cannot afford to fail. I have too many obligations and responsibilities.

Today, I am ready. Ready to accept what life places before me. I know I can do anything that's placed before me. God giveth and God taketh away and I must always remember that! All things, no matter what, cometh through Him.

Today, I am ready! I must draw from my past experiences and from those who were there for me. I must NEVER repeat history! Love, situations, people and circumstances that were not good for me is all included in the statement, "I must never repeat history", but I am ready to accept new challenges!

I am ready to pave another path in life's journey. A path never traveled before, but a path that shall be rewarding.

I am ready and my God will be with me every step of the way! I AM READY.

Today

Today my life must change. Change for the better and not for the worse.

Today, I look forward to challenging my mind, my heart and my soul because without a challenge... I am lost.

Today is what I make it to be. It's all up to me. Others can wish, pray and encourage me, but at the end of the day, it's all up to me.

Today will only come once and tomorrow is not promised. I will be judged by God if not by anyone else on this day. He gives me my strength, my love and He inspires me to move on. Today will only come once.

Today, as I prepare to face something new or something different, I must remember that someone has made a difference in my life never forgetting where I might be or might not be without those or someone who touched my life.

Today, I say to the world... I pray to my God to make me a better person and to forgive me for any wrong. Help me to say, "I'm sorry to anyone that I may have wronged and give me the strength to carry on no matter what."

Today, I create and tomorrow I will dream... Today, today, today!

I Am

I am, but who I am. I have tried to do what's right. I may have done some wrong, I may have walked over someone, I may have said something that was ugly, but I am who I am and with that... I ask God for forgiveness.

I am, but who I am as I walk this earth. There are things that I do not see. There are things that I close my eyes to because I didn't want to see, but I am who I am.

I am, but who I am... Does that mean, I cannot change? I can change and if change means I leave the not so good behind, then I must do just that! The good shall and will follow me the rest of my days!

I am, but who I am and this life will show me all the things that I have done. The good and the not so good and with that, "time brings about a change" and one day, I shall look back and see what life could have been like if I only had time to reflect back on these words, "if I could do it all over again, I would have done things differently." I am, but who I am, but with God's help, I will be a better person each day that I breathe God's fresh air.

Forty Years Ago

It was forty years ago in the dead of winter that a young beautiful girl fell in love. She was so beautiful, yet so young. But forty years later... that same beautiful girl is warm, charming and interesting. I will never forget that day. She warms my heart and can make the heart flutter like no other.

Life separated us for whatever reasons, yet she remains close in heart. Respect, I must. Never crossing the line because everything in life is timed.
She has a mind of her own and she is a real woman.
I can tell the story of a young girl who fell in love with me.
Forty years later.

It's All About You

It's all about you when it comes to Love. Your smile, your laughter and your interest. It's all about you when it comes to Life. Life, when filled with excitement brings about something real special. Special to feel, special to touch, but again, it's all about you.

It's all about you in a positive way because God gave you a gift to share with others and because you do it so well, I have to say again, "it's all about you."

It's all about you. Yet, you always keep others in mind. How sweet of you to think of others when others are thinking of you too. It's all about you. It's all about you in so many ways that time will not allow me to express all of them. But, as life would have it, never allow anyone to steal your joy because it's all about you when others are thinking of you too!

Life will always be about others and especially you too. It's all about you.

LIFE

(L)   Living to enjoy God's fresh air. Doing things that make living worthwhile. Living to love and living to give love as it is defined by you and only you.

(I)   Interesting is what this life is all about. There will be things, situations and life circumstances that brings about something interesting.

(F)   Fun to be in this world. Fun to create memories and especially good memories. Memories of friendship, companionship and many other aspects of life.

(E)   Excitement... without excitement in our life—life would be so dull. Dull to the soul, dull to the mind and dull to the heart. Life is supposed to be F-U-N and without fun, our life is done.

When this life is over or almost over, the mind will give you one last chance to look back and see what you may have done wrong or who you may have done something to and allow you to ask for forgiveness.

Either way, life is living; life is interesting; life is fun and life is excitement. Without those things, life is almost not worth living, but despite everything, just remember God is on our side no matter what!

In the end, life is what we choose to make of it!

JUST FOR YOU...

Today was an interesting day.

Someone beautiful studying to be a doctor came my way.

She was warm, polite, professional and caring too. You could tell she was sincere by the way she carried herself. Down to earth... that's what I say.

She'll be back in the morning is what she said. I'm not sure about her next move or what it might be, but you can bet...She'll be right on point.

Tomorrow she'll lay down the medical law to me. So my friend, get ready.

After all, she is someone beautiful studying to be a doctor. What else could a patient ask for? Just for You, I leave you with a smile.

LADY OF THE HOUR

Each day that you warm the halls,
Brings a smile or two, just a small
Reminder of you.
Travel the world they say, classic
Lady as you are, you are the lady of the hour.
Fresh as flowers, slim as can be, a
Personality that could only honor
the lady of the hour.

Sweet as can be, humble, kind, generous,
loving, soft spoken and well dressed.
The sexy sparkle of your eyes that strikes
With such sharpness that melts every
man's desires. She remains the lady of the hour.

Grateful I am, to know, to love, to share,
to wonder and to dream about no other,
but the Lady of the hour.

THOUGHTS OF YOU

I have thoughts of you daily.

Good thoughts, old thoughts

and new ones as well.

But, they are thoughts of you.

Thoughts of a moment here and there.

Thoughts of moments spent with you.

However so big or small, they are thoughts of you.

Thoughts of what could be, what might be or thoughts of what never will be.

But still they are thoughts of you.

Thoughts of pleasure, thoughts of happiness, thoughts of love, just thoughts of only you... just thoughts....

Thoughts of today-not thoughts of tomorrow...only my thoughts of you can begin to cultivate a dream of tomorrow.

My Thoughts of you are real, exciting, caring and loyal. Just thoughts...

Just thoughts can inspire a heart to pump, to beat an extra beat...but a pump or a beat is a thought of you.

Just a thought... live a little, explore a little, love a little, share a little, give a little and enjoy the moment. Just thoughts of you.

OH! WHAT A FLIGHT!

As I walked down the aisle, searching for a seat with many to choose from, out of nowhere, a beautiful brown tan woman appeared and I know oh what a flight it would be!

Slender and thin, froze my eyes did she and I knew I had to say hello and may I join you... without a doubt she replied, yes...hoping she would say, "yes my dear".

As the evening passed, the sun set and the clouds rose, I knew in my heart I was in for a time of my life, oh what a flight.

The warmth and tenderness of her smile, the style of her hair and the beauty of her fine tan legs made me say again, oh what a flight it would be.

A word here and a word there, drew me closer to fantasy in the sky. I knew right away, oh what a flight it would be.

As she departed, her words, her thoughts, her moves, her conversation lay embedded in my mind, heart and soul. Gone, she was just like that!!! Wondering if I would ever hear her voice.... To my amazement she came through. Oh what a flight it would be.

In the end, sweet as can be, she leaves me with sweet memories of what COULD never be, but her smile, her voice and her looks will always remind me of the woman from KC.

So take this with you my love, no matter where you go, a personality like yours and a smile like mine, placed together can only mean one thing... Oh what a flight it would be, as she disappears in the night. Oh! What a flight!

I Wish

I wish I could show you my true feelings.

I wish I could hold you for a few minutes in my arms so you could feel the love.

I wish I could spend time with you no matter how long or how short.

I wish I could look into your beautiful eyes and read what you might be thinking.

I wish things were different for us, yet somehow I believe we can adjust.

I wish I could show you if only briefly what fun we could have only,

if it creates everlasting memories.

I wish my love could extend beyond, today, tomorrow and forever,

but I know it is only for a little while.

I wish I could touch you deep inside and show you how passionate I am.

I wish I could do many things for you; to share my love, my thoughts and feelings for only

a little while.

I wish I could somehow have you say what you might be thinking.

I wish I could go on sharing my love with you, but I realize it takes two to tango and solo

is not the answer.

I wish I could be a star where my love would shine upon your heart day and night.

I just wish!

LADY OF MY DREAMS

We dream things that we often would like to come true... and the beauty of this dream...
is you.
I dream of you because of your body.
I dream of you because of your warmness.
I dream of you because I may not even have you, yet I still dream of you.

I dream because my God allows me to.
I dream of places I'd like to go with you and things I'd love to share.

I dream of the present and I dream of the future. Sometimes it's just to hold you, touch
you, see you or smell the scent of your beauty.

I dream not as a foolish dream, but of one who cares deeply and one who can see the snow
on the mountaintop and the wind blowing through the trees.

I dream hoping the good ones will come to pass to show the meaning of the heart, body,
mind and soul.

I dream, never giving up, hoping that one day a piece of one of my dreams will come true.

You will always remain the lady of my dreams. By day or by night... Don't ask me why because like dreams that come late into the night, it all reminds me of the beauty of you. My dreams of you are always a bright light.

I dream, I dream, I dream of the day or night that my love for you will somehow transpire into the love of a lifetime.

With all that said, I dream, I dream.
Sweet dreams and goodnight.

ASHLEY

Ashley, I saw you in my passing and I could not overlook your beautiful smile.

A smile of beauty… a smile of confidence, but a smile.

A smile that will make those you serve…smile.

A smile that warms the heart
A smile that shares just who you are…a smile.

A smile that defines a person that's not afraid to say what's on her mind.

A smile planted and a smile returned. That smile that will always remind me of you.

Yes, that smile!

The Reasons Why I Love You

There are many reasons why I love you…
It's not what might be, it's what I know could be.
It's not the dreams, it's the reality of you.
It's not the hopes of tomorrow…it's the hopes of today.
It's not wanting your every moment; it's wanting a little time.
These are a few of the reasons why I love you…

I can see the pleasure in your face, feel the effects in your hands…
I can see the need to want to overlook certain things, yet holding back just because…

Whatever the reason, the mind and heart is already seasoned to love you.
Just another reason why I love you.
It's not because I want to hold you, it's the need to love you.
It's not because I don't care, it's because I care too much…
Another proud reason to say, "I love you dear."

Time offers an opportunity…one that cannot be given back…
But one that brings memories on a card to the heart that reads
"Just another reason why I love you."

It's not the beauty of the eyes that I see. It's the look of contentment, the
look of joy, the sense of happiness and the willingness to want to give
it a try, holding back slowly builds the temptation to love…

Just another reason to give love a try.
We fail to see the sun for the clouds sometimes…
Yet the heart knows your lover's heart.

In the middle of the night, where there is no light…
thoughts of you guide me through the night.
And when daylight arrives, your love shines and shines…
Just another reason why I love you.

When it's all said and done, give love a try…
Love me long or love me short, either way
you can say, "you loved me and I loved you."

In the end, it's not what you could do for me;
it's what we did for each other.
It's not the sadness, the loneliness, the worries,
but the happiness that glows forever and forever…

Let's give it a try… even for a little while…
The heart says, "That's not too much to ask?"
These are only a few reasons of why

I LOVE YOU SO!
Let's give it a try.

My Love for You

My love for you is amazing; it's an amazing feeling just to love you. You amaze me every day in more ways than one. My love for you is unique. I have never loved like this before and will never love this way again. You are my first, my last and my everything.

My love for you is a constant reminder of how real love is supposed to be.
You are the first person I think about when I wake up every morning as well as the last person on my mind before I fall asleep at night.

My love for you is my joy and my happiness. You are my sunshine on a rainy day. You are my rainbow at that end of the storm. You are my beautiful snow angel made in the biggest snow storm. You are my north star leading me away from captivity. God truly blessed me when He sent you into my life.

My love for you is captivating. You have captured my heart, my mind, my body and my soul. Even if I had the key, I wouldn't remove the locks!

My love for you is something that will never change. We will make it together. I need you more than you will ever know. I promised to be loyal, to honor you and to always give my love to you and only you.

Every inch of me belongs to you. Without you in my life, it would be fruitless. I promise to never stop loving you. I believe that we were meant to be...you for me and me for you... forever and a day.

This is how many folks feel about real love.

Extra Special

I am extra special to myself, my brother, my sister, my parents, grandparents, friends, family and to God.

God made me extra special so I could see today and live for tomorrow. I must face whatever confronts me with a clear mind because God made me extra special.

God saw what I never could, but he allowed me to briefly understand why we are here on earth. I must find my reasons for His love and His teachings. My purpose in life was written by God and now I must find it and make the best out of it.
God made me extra special.

I'm extra special to my brother and sister. Our bond will grow stronger as we grow older. Our purpose in life will reveal itself as we live.

I am extra special because God made me and He made you. Don't ever allow anyone to make you think otherwise.

God made all of us and you are extra special because He loves all of us. You shall always be extra special.

Written by Grand P for my granddaughter, Sydney.

FAMILY

The word "family" means the world to almost all of us. Sometimes family means getting together, planning together, doing things together, praying together or just picking up the telephone and saying how are you doing?

Family to others just may mean having fun. Fun to just have fun…fun to plan together… maybe a card game, a vacation, a cookout or just fun to be around. This is what a true family is all about. Not where there are fake family members, fake friends or just fake, fake and fake… that's not the true meaning of family.

Family means to love each other. It means being there for each other and not trying to take advantage of anyone or a given situation.

Family means saying, "I love you brother, sister, uncle, aunt, nephew, cousin, sister-in-law, brother-in-law, mom or dad". Family sometimes is all that we have left in this world. Never forget the true meaning of family.

Sometimes we are faced with a different meaning of family. Whereas no one cares about anyone, but themselves. If the spotlight is not focused on them, then a barrel of confusion is coming your way.

Family of a different kind divides the true meaning of family and many, many folks suffer the effects of those others. Learn to enjoy family and be the one to say, "I am sorry".

Family sometimes is all that we have. Love and nurture family regardless of the situations or circumstances. Family is all that we have left sometimes.

The Path of Life

Each day that we are here on earth, we are faced with, "the path of life."
To some folks that path is a walk in the park and for others that path is an everyday struggle.

The path of life will carry us up hills, over mountains, down slopes and into valleys, but at the end of the day our path has carried us in a different direction. A different direction called the path of life.

The path of life could be about love, life, happiness, success or failures, but either way, we call this the path of life. Path of joy, path of happiness, path of sadness, path of desire, path of friendship, path of family and the path of being a child of God.

Choose your path of life with an open mind, a warm heart and with loving thoughts and for you, "the path of life" will be forever regarding the path of life that no one can take from you! Enjoy your path of life. Enjoy the Lord's blessing.

There Comes a Time in Our Life for Change

Sometimes, there comes a time in our life for change… we ponder about change. We think about change. We question ourselves about change and sometimes circumstances cause us to change. Either way, sometimes there comes a time in our life for change.

Change can be one of the hardest things to do and accept! We come to accept our being as what we are, but again, circumstance brings a change.

-A change in our beliefs… a change in our way of thinking.

-A change in the people we associate with… a change because change is necessary for whatever reason.

-A change to enrich our lives…a change because the same old scenery, brings about the same old results.

-A change because God loves us and we know right from wrong and because heaven is always a better place than earth.

-There comes a time in our life for change…just because.

I Need You

I need you not because of the meaning of the word...I need you because you are in my blood, in my heart and in my mind. I need you not because of my needs, but because of the way you treat me. The way you helped me expand my thoughts and ideals.

I need you not because I think of you often, but because of the things that you do for me, the things you try to do that's different from all others. I need you not because we are different, but because we came together as one; one with much love and affection. So, I will always need you forever my darling, "I NEED YOU".

Mindfulness of Thought

The thought process can be mindful. You have to put your thinking cap on to see the other side of the world. This side is rarely seen or experienced.

The thought process can play mind games on the mind. It goes from one direction to the other and back. It's amazing what the mind can say to the heart, body, mind and soul.

The thought process can be a mindful way of creating deep thoughts. Thoughts of today, thoughts of the moment and thoughts of the untold thoughts.

Always be mindful and the true meaning of, "mindfulness of thought". It can enlighten and uplift your heart, mind and soul.

If I Could Change Things I Would

If I could change things, I would because you deserve me and I deserve you.

If I could change things, I would...because you would get all my love and the kisses too... and not the few that I am limited to.

If I could change things, I would because real love is no joke, it has a price too. A price I'm willing to pay because of the love I have for you.

If I could change things, I would because in the end, it's only going to be just you and me.

If I could change things, I would because everything I do is for you, but in the end, it's all up to me and you.

THE DAY MY WORLD SLOWED DOWN

It was a cold January day in 2014 that my world slowed down. My body had been giving signals that something was wrong.

I made a call to see my doc, but I was convinced that I needed to come on to the E/R...that was the day my world slowed down.

Thinking I would be there for a while, however three days later, I am enjoying the view from 4 walls. Kind of reminds me of an inside cabin on Royal Caribbean. What a view.

The day my world slowed down, I had no other choice, but to give in. It was time for me to understand the signals and my pain.

Can't wait to get back on the move. Things to do and people to help. That's all I know. I am confident things will be alright. My purpose on earth is still not done.

The day my world slowed down will be a day that I shall never forget, but I am grateful for all the concerns and for all the professional care.

The day my world slowed down... a cold winter day that shall always be etched in my heart, my mind and my soul.

The Team

The word TEAM is defined differently by different people. On this day, I have the pleasure to share with you my thoughts on, "My Team".

The team, a group of medical professionals gathered together for a specific purpose. In my case... "The Team" was to determine the source of the "dropping heart" with some discomfort.

The team, made up of great minds with great expectations as they become great physicians in their own right!

The team, could not ask for much more. Dedicated to their OATH determined by any medical means necessary to find the cause.

The team looks out not only for me, but the many others who need their attention, their devotion and their wisdom as they travel the medical highway.

The team, I say, "thank you" in a big way for those who don't know how to express it and to those who do.

The team; Together-Engaged-Attentive-Motivated.

The team...may you enjoy a long enduring life in the field that you so love...Doctors.

How Long Will I Continue to Write?

How long will I continue to write? I don't know. This is a talent that my God giveth me and I must continue until there is nothing left for me to do.

I can't say for how long... because I really don't know. Writing is a way to share my thoughts, thoughts of others and a way for me to see things from my eyes.

I can't say for how long I will write, but what I do know is this...I must use this talent, no matter what.

There are things to tell. There are things left untold. There are things for the mind to wander and there are things again that must remain untold.
How long will I continue to write? You tell me.... Smile with love!

Life is Amazing

Life is amazing you see. Full of fun and full of joy. Things to see and things to talk about. It's amazing you see. Life is amazing, so much so that I really don't know where to begin. Shall I talk about me or shall I talk about you. Either way, life is amazing.

I am overly joyful when I see happiness all around the world. When I can feel the warmth of mankind. Just to know love is everywhere makes life a bit more amazing you see.

I hear tell of the poor who found wealth in a place not far from here. They shared their wealth with the world you see and again, life is amazing. There are many examples of how life is amazing, but I can only share one.

Rejoice in His name and pray every day for yourself and others in the world and you will find comfort in Him, so just relax and rejoice in His name. You too will feel His spirit and say, "life is amazing."

Life is amazing when God puts two people together for whatever reasons. Learn to enjoy each other, grow together, love together, build a foundation never built before and do something different. God put you together and God can pull you apart, but learn to understand each other and never forget life is indeed amazing.

Life is amazing when you feel love, when you see love and when you have someone who has touched your life like never before. Someone who has proven themselves to be different from all the others. Cultivate it to the fullest because real and true love can change you forever.

Life is amazing. Take this opportunity and do not let life or love slip away. For it may never come your way again.

Life is amazing and so are you!

Today's Fate

Today, we are faced with a difficult decision of innocent or guilty.
Today, we are asked to decide the fate of one man or woman.

Today, our thoughts are an open book to the judge, defense attorney, attorney general and the public. Today, we wait nervously as to whether our names will be called as a juror.

Today, the sun is out and we wait and we wait.

Today, we see faces never seen before and we see the expressions of what's next. Today, we listen to the judge as he gives instructions about this and that and what to do, not to do or what to say and what not to say.

Today in America...in Columbia, Tennessee, all of our Godly thoughts and beliefs are on display. Today, we listen to those picked for the jury and how emotional some get because today, we must choose. Today, we have no choice. Follow the judge's rules.
It's the law.

Jury Duty...Select Me If You May

Born in America where we know no wrong. Jury duty...select me if you may. Raised in an environment where color was an issue and law enforcement was our enemy. Jury duty select me if you may.

Taught right from wrong, tried to live by the Golden Rule, jury duty, select me if you may. Witnessed the mistreatment of the poor, disadvantaged and now watch how culture has become a hot topic. Jury duty, select me if you may.

America is no longer the melting pot for justice and equality. Jury duty, select me if you may. Reality TV, cops and the like has replaced good family values. Jury duty, select me if you may.

Politics has gotten personal, politicians are going to jail; race is still an issue, justice cannot truly be defined, equality of sentencing is out of the question...jury duty...select me if you may.

At the end of the day, please do not select me for jury duty. There is no justice in America.

The Blues

The blues has so many different meanings that it is hard to put into words. Blues is thought of in a way as a means of expressing something not so good in our life.

The blues sometimes will make a strong man weak...a determined woman soften her stance. The blues will bring back memories that will make you think... will it ever end, but that's another kind of blues.

Blues can express happiness because you are free from whatever held you in bondage. Blues of a happy nature can bring a smile to your face and joy to your heart because you can see the forest from the trees. You can see the sun from the clouds; you can see the rain drops from the storm, you can see reality from fantasy and you can see all of your past errors and now all you see is the beautiful bright sunshine.

The blues is just an expression of what we are going through or just what we have been through. "JUST THE BLUES."

Meet Me Halfway... Will You?

Meet me halfway, will you... really means that you have given your all and I do mean your all and now we are faced with a difficult decision of what to do next.

Sometimes things just happen. Sometimes without any explanation and we find ourselves trying to understand why or what happened. Yet, we are not ready to give up or to walk away... so as a last ditch effort, we say to that person, "meet me halfway... will you" hoping that a reasonable compromise can be worked out.

Sometimes as life would have it, we meet in the middle and try to resolve whatever it was that caused the ripple in our relationship. Sometimes, we walk away stronger than before and other times, we walk away knowing the end is near. Regrettably so, we must face the middle the same way that we must face the end, knowing we made an honest effort to mend our differences.

Meet me in the middle...will you, could mean many different things... Love, life, family, kids, friendship, a misunderstanding or something more exciting, either way, in order to compromise, we must meet in the middle and if not, just remember the end is near.

No matter what happens, enjoy life because we only pass this way once!
Enjoy life to the fullest knowing you tried.

Why We Met

No one really knows for sure why we met. Brought together because someone else thought of us, I suppose. Yet we have touched through our eyes, our voice and our adventure of what's next and why we met... maybe we saw that person who needed to be loved, touched or maybe needed a conversation or two. What remains is now that we have met what do we do?

Laugh, smile, share life experiences, dream about the future, wish for all the things we never had in a relationship and say to ourselves, "this can work with love, trust, faith, happiness and compassion" - then maybe we will understand why we met. Never letting go of what we really want, but only time will tell... and only then shall it be revealed... why we met!

Time

Time is often defined as the passing of a minute, hour, day, month or year.

During this passing time, some like myself, begin to think about a true soul mate.

One that we can laugh with.

One that we can cry with.

One that we can share happiness with.

One that will forever remain a part of one's life when life has expired.

Time sometimes can stop the world and often times, time is our best friend.

Either way, when one finds love with the meaning of a tomorrow, there is no time, just moments of joy.

It is often said, "I'll give you everything, everything that my God allows me to do."

Which includes precious time. Time spent with you is like true animation of what time can be like. Time is being together to share one's life.

Time can be one's best friend.

LIFE IS WHAT IT IS

We are born in this world in the imagination of God Almighty. Small as we may be, we grow, we learn, we communicate, we express and we share things. We share love, affection, caring and that great sense of belonging with love and happiness.

As we travel the by-ways of life, we experience…many experiences…some good and some not so good. We learn from self-preservation to protect ourselves as much as possible from the evils of the world.

One of our greatest assets are our warm smiles and warm hearts. However, we still learn to cultivate those important lessons of needs, wants, desires, love and affection to the point when we discover and realize what's right and what's not.

We learn to judge from one's actions coupled with a person's word. With those aspects, we pray along the way that God will give us strength to know and realize what's real and what's not. May we always strive for the joyous aspects of love, peace and happiness forever.

AGE

What is age...a number of hours, days, weeks, months that somehow counts our years on earth... but I ask what does age have to do with love?
Born by a difference in years should it matter? I say no.

Love is a universal act that bonds all minutes, hours, days, weeks and months into one.
I love you not because of age, but because of your commitment, your trust, your love, your thoughtfulness and most of all your respect... so I ask again... what does age have to do with it?
So what, we are seen differently by others, but does that matter... I say not...because love is a universal thing. It can make a sad heart happy and a smile shine from coast to coast.
Make a dream become reality...
Redefine the meaning of a soul mate.

Bring excitement to the soul and turn all past experiences into an everlasting peace of mind... so, I ask what does age have to do with it... when two people born in different years, yet they are brought together by the universal word Love... so I say to those born in a different year brought together by Love--- enjoy, enjoy and enjoy.

PARENT

I am parent, devoted to my son and my daughter. Maybe I was once married, separated, divorced or just a single parent by choice so I ask... is there love afterward... of course it is... shall I ask the question before I allow my heart to become involved... do you love kids or do you have any of your own...

His or her just reaction will reveal whether to open one heart to love or to reassess the many options life has to offer.
I'm single, but I tried. I once loved and I know I can love again, but to love me... you must love my kids... without them there cannot be we.

Single but Free, single in search for happiness, single with kids, sweetheart does not mean we can't be happy, it does not mean we cannot be one together.

Let's join hearts, minds, souls, and emotions and build our love, life, and our lives as parents sharing, the love and life that God has given us.

I am proud to be a single parent!

Nothing Changes

We go through our everyday living hoping that good things will happen to us as we emerge forward and sometimes nothing changes and we wonder why?

As we navigate left...right...forward... and backwards, some days nothing changes. We pray for a miracle to happen and it does and other times it does not. Nothing changes...

We give our best in everything that we do. From life, family, friends, employment, companionship, love and much more and nothing changes and we wonder why?

Life would have it that opposites attract and sometimes that can have a fatal ending. But not necessarily in death, but fatal in our relationship with that person of our dreams and our plans shatters into a million pieces and we ask why?

Sometimes, no matter what we do, how much we give, how much we cover up for them, how much we sacrifice, how much we care or even how much we love... nothing happens and we wonder why?

At the end of the day, just pray that one day something changes. Maybe the blinders will become eyeglasses; maybe the unknown becomes reality; maybe the written words become true spoken words and just maybe through it all... something changes.

Your Warmth

On yesterday you called me and we conversed about life in general, but at the end I could feel your warmth.

The first time I met you, your stern voice of concern, yet the softness of your words allowed me to know I could feel your warmth.
Months passed, years rolled by, our lives changed for one reason or the other, but I could still feel your warmth.

Tomorrow, next year or whenever our paths cross, I know in my heart, body and soul that I will always feel your warmth.

Warmth of kindness, warmth of gentleness, warmth of love, friendliness and determination shall always be a reminder of a "true" friend... and that shall always remind me of your warmth.

Printed in the United States
By Bookmasters